SITUATIONAL AWARENESS

The Urban Preppers Beginners Guide to Survival with Strategies and Essentials for Extreme Apocalyptic Disasters

NERO MAYO

First Printing, 2016

AUTHOR ABOVE

AUTHOR PAGE

Techyeah Productions
P.O. Box 6003
Portland, OR 97228

Before I dive in to the good stuff I want to be a little transparent. I don't just want to provide you one book that you download, and that is that. I want to have people, like you, that I notify when I'm putting out other valuable content. Your thinking, "what's in it for me?" Well, if you get a hold of it early it'll be free or reduced! This right-

About the Author

Nero Mayo is one of the multiple personalities of Bryan. Bryan is the Empire's Mastermind. The future Empire will create; Music and Movies, Kids T.V.-apps and much, much more. Nero Mayo publishes Ebooks on Kindle.

Author Central Page

Bryan, fresh out of the womb at 30-years-old has half the travelling experience already than half the people twice his age. He has done so many adventures he lost count at 3, but a small example of his time away from home involved travelling five days across the United States of America on a Greyhound bus (which he equates to breaking into the Professional Wrestling business), working on a Cruise line in Hawaii(which he equates to being taken hostage by a Sorority) and heading down under and working at a Grape Farm in Australia(which he equates to working at an Almond Factory in Australia). Besides "chillin' the freak out" Bryan loves self-expression through various mediums.

Table Of Contents

Introduction

Today, there are threats everywhere. Being aware of your surroundings is a must. This book will help you to understand the importance of situational awareness for your safety and the safety of your family.

What if the things go from bad to worst and the help you need didn't come as expected? It may sound harsh, but the reality of most crisis situations is that you're going to have to be your own first responder. When disaster hits, or when confronted with an unexpected threat, there's a very good chance you're going to have to survive on your own with only the knowledge and training you possess. With that in mind, how prepared are you to survive a real-life crisis situation? Or deal with the chaos that could ensue during the aftermath of a catastrophe?

The main purpose of this book is to motivate you to take action. To motivate you to put the right plans in place to see you through a crisis and ensure your ability to protect yourself and your family from a wide range of very real threats and disasters. By implementing the plans and strategies in this book, you will be able to survive many situations from short-term natural disasters to long-term economic problems, breakdowns in society and social unrest, and infrastructure failures or disasters.

Chapter 1: Understanding the Basic

What is Situational Awareness

Situational awareness-The unnatural ability to observe and analyze details about your environment is rudimentary for survival. Regardless of a wild animal attack, a violent person or natural disaster, this following guide will give you the basic understanding of situational awareness and how you can heighten your senses and prepare for the most unanticipated circumstances.

How it can save your life or your family's life

Having a presence of mind and complete awareness of your surroundings can save you and your loved ones. Having the ability to prepare for everything makes like activating an effective security system. Imagine having sensors placed at all access points (e.g., doors, windows, etc).

These sensors constantly signal their status - things like doors or windows opening, temperature, and movement - to a central control panel. Circuitry their evaluates all of the sensor alerts, determines which are normal and which are not, and, in the case of abnormal alerts, determines what action is warranted, and takes that action. In comparison, your senses (sight, hearing, touch, smell and taste) are reporting the world around you. Your mind processes those sensory inputs, determine which require your attention, then you decide and act.

The primary difference between you and an operational security system is in the attention-decision-act sequence. It's already hardwired into a security system - you have to learn what to do. Learning and practicing Situational Awareness is a very good place to start.

Preparing Your Self

To begin, you need to be prepared in every aspect of your personality. This is a must because your preparedness can make things better or can make things worse.

Mentally

This is the most important of preparation-preparing your mind. Not all people are aware but every one of us are equipped in surviving the harshest environments because it is hard wired in our brain. We just need to discover it. Unlocking your survival instincts helps you to create endless possibilities to help you and others in terms of unexpected disasters.

Self-awareness is the most essential part of mental preparation. Knowing your instincts on every situation helps you to focus on the present situation and survive any impending dangers.

Financially

You need also to be prepared financially. If things come to worse, you need to save cash for emergency situations. It is not enough that you are equipped mentally but you must also be equipped to have any cash at hand to spare.

It is a must to be prepared financially all the time. Banks and ATMs are not always around especially if you're stuck of the middle of nowhere or the place you got into doesn't accept credit cards transactions.

Physically

Physical fitness is the most important in any situational awareness preparation. Basic skills and training in surviving imminent situations are a must so you need to check if you are physically capable of the physical expectations one might require if you find yourself in a "survival mode" situation Some questions to ask yourself when determining this:

- How flexible am I? Can I tie my own shoes?
- Can I touch my toes without bending my knees?
- What type of range do you have in your shoulders?
- Have you had surgeries that limit your mobility?
- What about your strength?
- Can you lift heavy stuff?
- Do you have back problems that prevent you from lifting?
- How is your endurance? If you had to run from a crazy machete swinging maniac how far could you run before you lose your breath and get caught? Maybe running a 5k or 10k a few times a year can help you in this area?

Assess your surroundings with your senses

Situational awareness includes all the resources to assess your surroundings to any possible threats. This also includes all your senses like smell, taste or even touch. This is a part of our instincts to detect any impending dangers in our surroundings. So it greatly helps to develop self-awareness to be able to incorporate survival skills effectively.

Man developed survival instincts as a results of millions of years of evolution. You may not be aware but your instincts tell you if there are any impending dangers to your surroundings. There is an effective method to develop this instinct and this is called the OODA loop (Observe, Orient, Decide, and Act).

OODA Loop

This method is an effective way to develop your senses in any situation possible. The OODA acronym stands for:

OBSERVE – sensing (seeing, hearing, touch, and to a lesser degree smell and taste) what is occurring in your environment.

ORIENT – consciously focusing your attention on those sensory inputs that are relevant to you.

DECIDE – analyze and decide on a course of action based on your perceptions - and your beliefs.

ACT – immediately acting on your decision.

As mentioned, OODA is a loop. In the first iteration of the loop, you have taken some action. Your situation has just changed. The other players in your relevant event will be adjusting their loop to accommodate your changes. Therefore, it is now necessary to go through the loop again, taking both your changes and the changes of your surroundings, into consideration. These changes lead you to a new decision and a new action...and another new loop. This process continues until the relevant event has run its course. The changes you make in your loop are your efforts to change the outcome of the relevant event in your favor.

When in a relevant event, your possible actions fall into three categories: escape, evade, or engage. Your best choice by far is to escape. If you cannot escape, then you evade; that is, seek cover or concealment If and only if you cannot evade, then you must engage your attacker – and you only do so until you can evade, and you only evade until you can safely escape.

Finally, you should be aware that through the study and practice of situational awareness, you will experience a change in behavior – you will become sensitized to a lot more of the activity that is constantly occurring around you. Over time, it will become second nature and you will be continuously active.

The observational element of OODA requires, by far, the most significant changes in behavior. It also represents the largest amount of time to learn and perfect, and is to be practiced continuously.

Chapter 2: Knowing Your Survival Plan

Understanding What to Prepare For

Understanding the nature of every threat is a must in order to create your survival plan. To begin, you need to understand the exact types of disasters and threats you're potentially going to face. This may sound a little simplistic, but not all disasters are created equal. What works in one situation, or in one area of the world, may not work when you factor in specific location-based threats.

While some of the supplies, techniques, and skills you need to survive may overlap, to be truly prepared for any situation you need to know exactly what type of disasters you're preparing for and what problems you'll most likely encounter as a result of that specific disaster.

That work starts with identifying the most likely threats you'll face based on your geographical location, your lifestyle, and a number of other factors that will be unique to your specific situation. The following section will help you get started with your preparedness planning.

Threats; what are these?

Knowing your surroundings and understanding what are the proper actions or behaviors to do in any imminent situation is a must in order to survive. To do this you must know how to assess any threats that may come your way. A threat assessment helps you visualize what threats you'll face, scrutinize known risks related to the threat, strategically evaluate your response, and helps you start to identify the specific steps you need to take to stay safe. It's going to help you protect the people you love from harm.

- Make a realistic list of what the most likely threats are and how the threats will affect you should you face them. This should be a location-specific list; if you live in the Mojave Desert, hurricanes probably shouldn't be on the list. That being said, when traveling to a new area on vacation, I always do a mini threat assessment before arriving-and leaving.
- Under each threat, make a list of your vulnerabilities based on that specific threat. What problems do you foresee happening when the threat strikes? Think about disaster-specific threats as well as threats that may come from how people react to the disaster.
- Do you or anyone in your family have any personal considerations that could be exacerbated due to each of the identified threats? These can include medical conditions, age-related limitations, mobility issues, or specific dietary needs that might be hard to meet during a disaster.
- After the initial threat has passed, are there any threats you expect to spring up as a result of the disaster? These can include power outages, looting, home invasions, or anything that may be specific to your location. For instance, if you live near a nuclear reactor that could be affected by the initial disaster, this would definitely be a threat you need to list. Consider what happened as a result of the Japanese earthquake/tsunami that crippled Japan's Fukushima Daiichi nuclear reactors.

Knowing Different Threats in Your Surroundings

Location-based threats may not be immediately apparent, but I bet there're more potential threats in your neighborhood than you've probably considered.

- Is there anything about your town that makes you a likely terrorist threat? This can be anything from a large population base to military bases or chemical plants that can be easily targeted.
- Do you know what types of chemicals local businesses use in their production processes? Industrial accidents can have devastating effects on neighboring communities.
- Do you live in a flood zone or an area that's at higher risk for a specific type of natural disaster?
- Do you know about local crime patterns or have any idea of how many local gangs are in your area? Chicago has ~20 gang related homicides every weekend.*

The first step in minimizing your threat for a hazard is awareness. You need to take a serious look at your immediate area and figure out what potential dangers exist.

Deadly chemicals, flammable and explosive substances, and even radioactive materials are shipped daily on the nation's highways and railways. Most chemical accidents are caused by transportation accidents. Even people living in the most remote areas of the country cannot completely isolate themselves from danger. In fact, if you live anywhere near a highway or a railway, there's a pretty good chance you have hazardous chemicals traveling through your area on a regular basis.

It's estimated that in the United States alone, some 4.5 million facilities either store or use hazardous chemicals and materials. Many of these facilities are allowed to operate in or near residential areas, where a hazardous material accident or chemical spill could quickly overtake a neighborhood.

From obvious places like industrial plants and chemical waste sites to not-so-obvious places like hospitals, dry cleaners, and food processing plants, you need to be aware that hazardous material accidents can happen anywhere.

Most communities have Local Emergency Planning Committees that are responsible for knowing what chemicals are being used in a community and developing plans to deal with emergencies involving those chemicals. Your local Emergency Planning Committee should be able to provide you with this information and is the first place I would start. These committees are usually run by local government officials and/or local fire or law enforcement departments.

Find out what chemicals are being used near your home, and find out what plans and warning systems are in place.

Besides being an obvious terrorist target, almost one-third of U.S. dams are over fifty years old, the average lifespan of most dams. Even more troubling is the fact that somewhere around fourteen thousand dams are classified as high-hazard, meaning that any operational mistake could cause a significant loss in human life; two thousand are so bad that they have been rated structurally deficient, meaning they are at a high risk for failure.

Most Americans are unaware of the problems and don't even realize their homes lie directly in the path of an inundation zone. Because the government restricts most maps from showing inundation zones, check with your state's dam safety agency or talk to local emergency management officials about potential dangers.

Chapter 3: You're Survival Tools

Memorization techniques

Using Your Memory skills as often as you can, could be helpful in improving your retention abilities and cognitive processes. There are many exercises you can do enhance your memory skills. Some are listed here for you to try.

Active Imagination

Active Imagination is one of the exercises you should try in order to enhance your memorization skills. Visualization is a great memory exercise. You may have used it at birthday parties as a child when asked to memorize several objects before they are hidden. You would then be asked to repeat the names of the objects for a prize.

You can do this while going about your everyday life. While standing in the supermarket queue, visualize what is in your shopping basket without looking at it. Alternatively, focus on your bedroom at home and force yourself to remember all the things that are in it. In time, you will hopefully become more observant and, as a result, will be less likely to forget things. The goal here is to really hone in on enhancing your memory skills. The more frequent you practice memorization the better you will be at active imagination.

Reiteration

Reiteration or repeating words over and over is also another memory exercise. For example, on your way to work, repeat the list of things that you need to do. Then when you get into work, you can systematically through your memory practice and preparation, proactively resolve each task before you forget.

The same trick can be used when going shopping. Repeat the list of things you need to purchase and you'll find it easier to remember when you get there. Over time you will ideally build up enough practice to be able to apply this to addresses and phone numbers and eventually longer forms like medications and directions.

You may also find that you are more likely to remember appointments if you repeat things back to the person arranging them. So when someone says, "see you at 4pm on Tuesday at Starbucks on Mill Plane Road?" You then reply with repeating the WHOLE thing back focusing on the two (or sometimes three) main points. "I will see you at **4pm**, this **Tuesday** at the **Starbucks on Mill Plane Road**" This is also a great activity to practice when meeting someone new and you have trouble remembering their name.

Games Improve Your Memory

Did you know that gaming has a benefit in improving your memory skills? This of course is different than enjoyment and entertainment? New computer-based memory games are constantly coming out, but you don't need to spend a fortune – you will even be able to find plenty of games online that are free. If you do decide that you want to invest in a good memory game, you could try the **Posit Science Brain Fitness Program**, which will provide you with exercises that become increasingly harder, causing your brain to expand and grow wrinkles!

Language Improvement

Learning a new language improves the connections of neurons in your brains which thus sharpen your memory. It may seem like a tall order to learn a language-just to improve your memory and although learning a language is time-consuming, if you are able to pick up another language, it will reward you handsomely. Consider the following though, you don't need to commit "full-time" both in time and resources to learn the basics of a language. The quickest way is to be around the individuals whose language you wish to learn. Want to learn Spanish? Watch Telemundo. Want to learn French? Watch Michael Gondry documentaries.

You may even decide to learn just a few words in a number of languages. Doing this with children is a great way to turn language learning into a game and you can even test each other on how much you can remember. If you have a poor memory, the easiest way to improve it is to fix your diet and drink more water. I'm almost 100% positive that your diet could use improvement. Shoot, even mine could-everyone can.

Having proper nutrition and enough electrolytes allow your brain to function properly. Imagine trying to drive a car without gas or oil. Yeah, you won't get far. Starting with your diet will be a game changer in of itself. However, simple exercises can also be of great help, provided that you do them on a daily basis. If you train your brain to do them without thinking too hard about it, you should soon see the benefits.

Baselines, Goals, and Action plans.

Behavioral Change

As mentioned above, good situational awareness practices **have** to be learned. They require a certain amount of effort and they require continual practice to refine. They begin with the active decision to change behavior. Good situational awareness happens because of a conscious decision. Frankly, it takes work - and time. You must decide if you are willing to commit your energy to the process. This is about the classic Tony Robbins quote "You have the power within you right now, to change." Every change begins with a decision to change. This is where it begins. Your initial mindset is what is the game changer here. Before you even begin you are deciding if you are going to make change and your chance of succeeding at it is already determined before you even begin. This is your mindset.

Self-Defense

This relates to what actions you are willing to take to preserve your safety. There is what is known as a Force Continuum. It ranges from:

DO NOTHING - provide no resistance and accept whatever the situation presents to you.

AVOID - the beginnings of resistance. Taking action to avoid a relevant event before it occurs or during the event, when an opportunity presents itself.

HURT - resist by means of force - to the extent that you cause enough pain to your attacker that you have the opportunity to evade or escape.

INJURE - higher resistance, to the extent that your adversary is temporarily incapacitated, allowing you to escape.

MAIM - higher resistance, to the extent that your adversary is permanently incapacitated.

LETHAL FORCE - highest resistance, to the extent that you believe that you, your family, or whoever you protect are in imminent danger and you must take whatever action is needed to protect them or yourself. This could include lethal force.

Hone your observation skills by playing the A-game (Awareness game)

You can even train your kids (and yourself) to be more observant by playing the "A-Game," or Awareness Game.

This game is simple for example, if you're going to work observed your surroundings carefully. Identify the different details of the colors of the buildings, how people are walking there, what time they are passing on the particular street and many more.

This way you can enhance your self-awareness on your surroundings and learn to identify any threats that may follow and familiarized yourself around you.

Three things to regularly exercise when you find yourself in a new environment is to remember the rules of three. Find three people, remember three one word characteristics that describe them and three mannerisms they exhibit. For example; Tall, black, bald-clears throat excessively, big strides, head tilted.

Behavioral Cluster

Observing behavior of others is an essential part in creating your survival plan. This is similar to the Awareness game. Normally people try to socialize with others without imposing any threats. But sometimes people are acting suspicious in ways that cause threats to others. Below are some behaviors to look for in order to deal with properly.

Dominance/Submissive behaviour

People are normally friendly to each other then act submissively to show that they are accommodating. But in some instances people get a dominant behaviour especially if they have high self-esteem or somewhat over confidence.

This often cause them to be pushy and bossy to others and often times aggressive. This is a behaviour to lookout for in order to be prepare in case that a conflict might occur.

Comfortable/uncomfortable behaviour

People are normally comfortable with each other in the sense that they have nothing to worry about(generally) or threat apprehension beforehand. But when you observe that some people are uncomfortable for no reason at all, this might be a threat. People who look often at their surroundings (eyes darting, not making eye contact) are often questionable threats thus making us uncomfortable-so self-awareness is a must. This behaviour is also apparent in someone who is psychotic or has a form of psychosis. So be aware that it is possible that you will see this and it's nothing worthy of a YouTube video.

This also applies the other way around. If you feel that the particular situation is safe/comfortable yet you see specific people obviously being suspicious, then it's important to acknowledge your comfort level. This also imposes a potential threat to watch for. Potential threat, just be aware.

Interested/uninterested behaviour

Normally people are not interested in their surroundings for any number of reasons. Some are caught in their own situations. Others are focused on the particular object of interest. Some don't care at all. One thing I have noticed from working in Hospitals, Restaurants, Mills, Cruise lines ect; is that when someone is not acknowledging you or they aren't being friendly, 99% of the time it's something about them. Many people these days are SO focused on their own little world that most of the time someone's attitude is about them in their head, their own little bubble.

But if you observed someone who took interest in the particular person or object which doesn't make any reasonable sense at all, this must be taken as precaution of your surroundings.

Other behavioral threat indicators

• Marine combat Profilers

These are people who are taught to look out for behaviors that could indicate a threat and apply it to civilian situations in addition to the three behaviors listed above.

Shifty hands

This practice is often observed by law enforcement and military officers by checking the hands of any person they engage. There are two reason for these. First is to ensure that the particular person doesn't hold anything that could cause harm to that particular person ie; a weapon.

Second reason is often times hands send visual signals. This could be someone with sweaty palms, or dry clammy hands. Either of those would indicate nervousness to some degree. Why would someone's hands be sweaty...? They are about to lunge at you because they think you are Batman.

Acting Natural

These are people who are often acting normal under the circumstances which they are intended to do otherwise. They are often trying hard to do that particular activity in order to deceive other people. An expert can easily detect these people when they often exaggerate their actions with the intention to deceive thinking those particular actions they're expected to do-are exhibited subtly.

Have a plan of action based on what you observe

Developing a plan depends on what you observe in your surroundings. You need a thorough analysis and to ask yourself relevant questions to arrive on the right plan.

When it comes to surviving a disaster, the single most important thing you can do is have a plan. Planning helps take the stress out of the situation and allows you to tackle it with a clear and focused mind, which is vitally important to your survival.

Survival situations can create unimaginable amounts of stress, severely compromising your ability to think clearly and take decisive actions. Creating a well-thought-out plan before the crisis hits can often be the determining factor in your ability to survive that situation.

Situational Awareness is a Preventative Tool

Prevention is better than cure as the old saying goes. Situational awareness helps you to prepare in every situation. That will go a long way thus making you more equip as the emergency called for an immediate action.

Practice Practice Practice

Practice makes perfect. Practicing self-awareness in every situation helps you optimize your presence of mind and concentration. Visualizing also helps. Visualize successful situations. Imagine scenarios and how they would unfold. Then, see yourself going through the effective steps to escape the circumstance. Our minds don't know the difference between real life and what we "see" in our minds. So having the practice "mentally" of surviving a compromising situation will actually benefit you as it will register in your mind as success. This will boost your confidence in your survival skills and it will have secondary benefits as well.

Chapter 4: Other skills

These survival skills are important because they will help you survive should disaster strike. All of these skills are necessary to maximize the probability of your survival. Fundamental basics to ensure your survival should be your main focus and take away from this Ebook.

Ignite to Live

Building a fire is essential to cook, boil water, produce heat, produce light or signal for "help" via smoke (burning wet wood will produce a considerable more amount of smoke).

In order to build a fire, you will collect dry wood and tinder (smaller shrubbery that aids in building a flame) to build a fire. You can use a saw or axe to cut or your studly arms to collect wooden branches that can easily catch fire. Make sure to clear the ground and collect debris and grass to burn and reduce the fire from getting out of control.

The fire requires oxygen and it is important for you to build an air flow into the ignition. Proper air flow. This is if you don't have a lighter or matches and your starting your fire by rubbing two sticks together like a Caveman. The fuel will actually burn in the fire and you can use branches, sticks and splinters to stoke the fire once it starts.

You will need an ignition source too, such as matches, lighter, fire starter, etc. You can also use stones to ignite the fire. But seriously...who doesn't carry a lighter on them or have matches around the house?

You can also build an upside down the fire by keeping large logs and fuel wood in a bottle with tinder and kindling at the top. If you use a metal water bottle you could use this as a fire for cooking (only if you have NO other option).

Basic Water Purifier

Water has a higher priority ranking than food, because you can exist for longer amount of time without food (about three weeks) than you can without water (about three days – and that's pushing it!) Many different aspects of water will be covered in this section, from collecting and storing to purifying and recycling.

You can boil water to purify it because it is one of the easiest ways to remove impurities from water. You can also make a solar still in the area where the sunlight is good for this work.

Take a bowl or a container to hold water and keep it on a flat surface. Take a weighted cup and keep it on the flat part of the bowl and it should be heavy enough to stand still on the surface of the water. Pour dirty water in the bowl, but avoid putting it in the cup.

Place wrap on the top of the bowl and seal it completely. Keep a rock on the top of the clear wrap where the cup is placed. Keep the bowl in the sun so that the sun can evaporate the water and the wrap can protect it from escaping. The water will go to the weighted part with the rock and start dripping into the cup. No water will leave the bowl and the clean water will be in the cup. This procedure may take hours or even days.

Learn what to eat

Learning what to eat is necessary in order to survive when disasters strikes. You can look up Foraging This will tell you what is safe and and how to go about picking wild plants. You can harvest anything that is available, but it's imperative that you understand what is safe to harvest. It will be good to learn some harvesting skills because these will help you to get numerous items for food. You can use a honey bee's hive to get honey. To remove honey bees from the hive, make sure to wear protective clothes and use smoke or fire to get to the hive without disturbing the bee's.

Learn about the types of animals in your area and try to get some good details about their inhabitants. You should learn about animal traps and snares because these will help you to hunt small animals and birds for food. You can keep a slingshot so that you can target birds and small animals. Keep a fishing rod and a bow and arrow with you to catch fish and other mammals, such as rabbits. Drift nets, fishing lines and balloons can also help you to trap fish for food. You should learn how to prepare whatever it might be you plan on hunting.

Other Survival skills

Having A Swiss Knife

A good knife with a fixed or folding blade will help you to carve wood and cut small branches. It is good in the skin and gut game, preparation of food, traps and snares, and for your self-defense. The fixed blade should be durable enough because it can be used for various tasks. It is a versatile option and maneuverable allows it to handle lots of tasks. Clean it after it's use and then apply some grease on its surface to keep it secure from rust and dust.

The small knife is extremely important because it helps you to do numerous precision dependent jobs that are difficult to handle with a large blade. You can keep a small, medium and large knife to handle numerous tasks efficiently.

Chapter 5: Surviving the Unexpected

Surviving Natural Calamities

Natural calamities are threats that are caused by natural forces like thunderstorms, tornados, tsunamis, earthquakes and volcanic eruptions. Surviving these events you need enough preparation and presence of mind in order to avoid errors that may cause more inconvenience and in order to save time and lives of others.

Below are some tips that you can use in surviving these natural calamities.

- Avoid touching any electrical appliances that are not attached to surge protectors. Even then you still need to be cautious.
- If driving, look for the safest place to pull off the road. Park and turn on your vehicle's emergency lights. Stay in your vehicle, unless you can safely make your way into a sturdy building.
- Listen to your NOAA Weather Radio or local news for storm-related updates.
- If you can hear thunder, you are technically in the danger zone. When lightning is in the area, there really is no safe place outdoors. As soon as you hear the rumble of thunder, it's time to take shelter and head indoors.
- If you're outside and cannot make it to a safe shelter, take cover in a low-lying area and minimize contact with the ground. Avoid hilltops, open fields, water, high ground, and tall, isolated trees.
- Avoid contact with metal objects such as fences, bleachers, golf clubs, fishing poles, or anything that can attract lightning.

- Put together an emergency kit/bug out bag that's filled with the supplies you need to survive an extended disaster.
- Firmly secure large appliances, water heaters, heavy objects, mounted televisions, and anything that can fall and cause injury during a quake. Most home improvement stores sell earthquake straps, bolts, and other stabilizing equipment.
- Remove any large items that are near your bed such as mirrors, picture frames, and artwork.
- Install safety latches on cabinets to prevent them from opening during a quake.
- Have an evacuation plan in place that includes a way to contact everyone in your family should the quake hit when you're separated.
- Practice your emergency evacuation plan on a regular basis. Everyone in your family should know exactly what to do when disaster strikes.
- Keep your cell phone nearby at all times and make sure it's always sufficiently charged.

Surviving Man-Made Threats

Preparing and surviving man made threats is something to plan-you must take a proactive approach to prepare and is a good start because there has been such an increase in terroristic attacks. It doesn't help that we have become so dependent on technology. The way we live, travel, and rely on modern technology has left us incredibly vulnerable to all sorts of manmade disasters and threats. All it takes is one event to disrupt our way of life and cause an unthinkable amount of turmoil.

From nuclear and biochemical terrorist attacks to vital infrastructure shutdowns and cyber-attacks, the world is facing a frightening number of manmade disasters that were once unimaginable.

- Avoid championship games at any type of sporting event. It's sad but people seem to have a hard time controlling themselves at these types of events; throw a couple of hours of drinking into the mix and it's pretty easy to predict what's going to happen.

- Stay away from any type of social justice rally especially if it's a rally to protest a prior act of violence. Ironically, these types of rallies often have a way of inciting even more violence and can quickly get out of control.
- Immediately take shelter, preferably in a basement or underground concrete shelter. If that's not available, find anything that adds some sort of mass between you and the external threat.
- Turn off any kind of air conditioning or air-driven heating units and seal up the vents using plastic sheeting and duct tape from your stockpile.
- Seal all windows and doorways with plastic sheeting and duct tape, and stay indoors for at least forty-eight hours.
- Listen to local news reports, and try not to leave your shelter until the all clear has been given.
- It may also be a good idea to keep air purification equipment due to the possibility of a biochemical attack.

Conclusion

Situational Awareness is a must nowadays especially when there are very few safe places. This book relies so much on the present situation where people need to be more aware of their surroundings in order to protect themselves against any threats that may affect themselves and their family.

This book will greatly impact your level of presence. It's designed as a guide to prepare yourself for the unimaginable. It's imperative that you create an effective plan to survive disaster. Remember, the key to surviving any type of disaster is doing your own research, identifying the most likely threats, and then doing everything you can to prepare for those threats. The choice of what you do with the information provided in this book is yours, but at the very least, consider the threats that are outlined and then figure out how you would respond to those threats in a way that ensures your survival.

Review Page

Thank you very much for purchasing my book.

I strive to make my future books better than the previous ones and one of the quickest ways to improve them is with feedback. Thank you in advance for your feedback.

About the Author

Nero Mayo is fresh out of the womb, 30-years-old-with half the travelling experience already than half the people twice his age. He has done so many adventures he lost count at 3, but a small example of his time away from home involved travelling five days across the United States of America on a Greyhound bus(which he equates to breaking into the Professional Wrestling business), working on a Cruise line in Hawaii(which he equates to being taken hostage by a Sorority) and heading down under and working at a Grape Farm in Australia(which he equates to working at an Almond Factory in Australia). Besides "chillin' the freak out" and "you know...chillin'," Nero loves self-expression through various mediums.

Free Offer

I want to thank you again for checking out my book. I look forward to providing you with more information that you can benefit from. Like I said at the beginning I want to have awesome people like you, that I notify when I'm putting out other valuable content! Check out my Author central page to join my email list and get these rewards!

www.ingramcontent.com/pod-product-compliance
Lightning Source LLC
Chambersburg PA
CBHW071310280526
45788CB00004B/1871